If Found Return To:

Name:..

Address: ....

Mobile: ....

In Case of Emergency

Name:..

Mobile: ....

INTRODUCTION

Welcome to TrailGenius, your comprehensive companion for documenting and reflecting on your hiking adventures! This hiking logbook has been thoughtfully designed to help you capture every detail of your journey, from the specifics of each trail to your personal observations and experiences.

In this logbook, you'll find dedicated spaces to record essential information such as date, day, location, trail name, and terrain type. To make your entries more detailed and informative, we've included fields for start latitude and longitude, weather icons to represent various conditions, temperature, and wind. You can also indicate if the day felt warm, cold, or mild, adding a personal touch to your notes.

To help you keep track of your progress, there are sections for start and end time, duration, distance, elevation, and the type of route you took. You can also list your companions, making it easy to remember the people who shared your journey.

Throughout the logbook, you'll find prompts for interesting sights and questions to consider while you journal, encouraging you to engage more deeply with your experiences and the natural world around you. These prompts will inspire reflection and spark memories of the challenges you overcame, the beauty you witnessed, and the personal growth you achieved on the trail.

TrailGenius is designed to be more than just a logbook—it's your personal guide, inviting you to immerse yourself in the world of hiking, explore new paths, and create lasting memories. As you fill these pages with your unique stories, you'll discover a deeper connection to nature, your fellow hikers, and yourself.

Happy hiking!

Goal Setting & Achievements

Use the lists below to help you start your goals, how will you achieve them? You may have different goals, these are just suggestions.

Fitness & Endurance

- Increase hiking distance
- Improve hiking speed
- Hike for multiple days
- Complete a hike with significant elevation gain
- Build stamina for longer hikes

Skills & Knowledge

- Learn navigation skills
- Become proficient in first aid
- Study local flora and fauna
- Understand trail maintenance
- Leave No Trace principles
- Improve photography skills

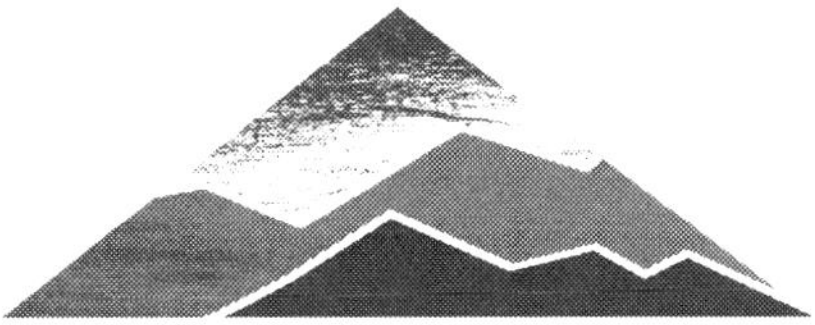

Exploration & Adventure

- Hike a specific bucket-list trail
- Explore a new national park
- Complete a trail in another country
- Hike in different seasons
- Participate in a hiking event or group hike.

Personal Growth & Reflection

- Connect with nature
- Find mindfulness through hiking
- Challenge personal limits
- Journal consistently about hiking experiences
- Share hiking stories with others.

A journey of a thousand miles
begins with a single step

- Laozi

Hiking Log

Hike Details

Day/Date: ....

Location: ....

Trail: ....

Terrain: ....

Start - Latitude: ....

Longitude: ....

Weather

Feel

☐ Warm ....

☐ Cold

☐ Mild ....

Rating: ☆ ☆ ☆ ☆ ☆

Difficulty:

Time - start : .... end : .... expected finish: ....

Duration: .... **Distance:** ....

Elevation: ....

Route Type: ☐ Circular ☐ Out-and-Back ☐ Point-to-Point

Companions: ....

....

Interesting Sights

....

....

....

....

....

....

Reflections for Journal

What was the most challenging part of the hike?

How can I better prepare for this next time?

How did I feel physically and mentally during the hike?

Was there anything I wish I had brought or anything that was unnecessary?

Did I set any goals for myself during the hike, and did I achieve them?

Journal / Notes

Snapshot or Trail Doodle

Hiking Log

Hike Details

Day/Date: ....

Location: ....

Trail: ....

Terrain: ....

Start - Latitude: ....

Longitude: ....

Weather

Feel

☐ Warm ....

☐ Cold

☐ Mild ....

Rating: ☆ ☆ ☆ ☆ ☆

Difficulty:

Time - start : .... end : .... expected finish: ....

Duration: .... Distance: ....

Elevation: ....

Route Type: ☐ Circular ☐ Out-and-Back ☐ Point-to-Point

Companions: ....

....

Interesting Sights

....

....

....

....

....

....

Reflections for Journal

What was the most challenging part of the hike?

How can I better prepare for this next time?

How did I feel physically and mentally during the hike?

Was there anything I wish I had brought or anything that was unnecessary?

Did I set any goals for myself during the hike, and did I achieve them?

Journal / Notes

Snapshot or Trail Doodle

Hiking Log

Hike Details

Day/Date:..

Location:..

Trail:..

Terrain:..

Start - Latitude:..

Longitude:..

Weather

Feel

☐ Warm ....

☐ Cold

☐ Mild ....

Rating: ☆ ☆ ☆ ☆ ☆

Difficulty:

Time - START :.................. END :.................. EXPECTED FINISH:................

Duration:.................. **Distance:**..................

Elevation:..

Route Type: ☐ Circular ☐ Out-and-Back ☐ Point-to-Point

Companions:..

....

Interesting Sights

....

....

....

....

....

....

Reflections for Journal

What was the most challenging part of the hike?

How can I better prepare for this next time?

How did I feel physically and mentally during the hike?

Was there anything I wish I had brought or anything that was unnecessary?

Did I set any goals for myself during the hike, and did I achieve them?

Journal / Notes

Snapshot or Trail Doodle

Hiking Log

Hike Details

Day/Date:..

Location:..

Trail:..

Terrain:..

Start - Latitude:..

Longitude:..

Weather

Feel

- ☐ Warm ....
- ☐ Cold
- ☐ Mild ....

Rating: ☆ ☆ ☆ ☆ ☆

Difficulty:

Time - start :.................. end :.................. expected finish:..................

Duration:.................. **Distance:**..................

Elevation:..

Route Type: ☐ Circular ☐ Out-and-Back ☐ Point-to-Point

Companions:..

....

Interesting Sights

....

....

....

....

....

....

Reflections for Journal

What was the most challenging part of the hike?

How can I better prepare for this next time?

How did I feel physically and mentally during the hike?

Was there anything I wish I had brought or anything that was unnecessary?

Did I set any goals for myself during the hike, and did I achieve them?

Journal / Notes

Snapshot or Trail Doodle

Hiking Log

Hike Details

Day/Date: ....

Location: ....

Trail: ....

Terrain: ....

Start - Latitude: ....

Longitude: ....

Weather

Feel

☐ Warm ....

☐ Cold

☐ Mild ....

Rating: ☆ ☆ ☆ ☆ ☆

Difficulty:

Time - start : .... end : .... expected finish: ....

Duration: .... **Distance:** ....

Elevation: ....

Route Type: ☐ Circular ☐ Out-and-Back ☐ Point-to-Point

Companions: ....

....

Interesting Sights

....

....

....

....

....

....

Reflections for Journal

What was the most challenging part of the hike?

How can I better prepare for this next time?

How did I feel physically and mentally during the hike?

Was there anything I wish I had brought or anything that was unnecessary?

Did I set any goals for myself during the hike, and did I achieve them?

JOURNAL / NOTES

SNAPSHOT OR TRAIL DOODLE

HIKING LOG

HIKE DETAILS

DAY/DATE:..

LOCATION:..

TRAIL:..

TERRAIN:..

START - LATITUDE:..

LONGITUDE:..

WEATHER

FEEL

☐ WARM ....

☐ COLD

☐ MILD ....

RATING: ☆ ☆ ☆ ☆ ☆

DIFFICULTY:

TIME - START :.................. END :..................... EXPECTED FINISH:................

DURATION:.................. DISTANCE:..................

ELEVATION:..

ROUTE TYPE: ☐ CIRCULAR ☐ OUT-AND-BACK ☐ POINT-TO-POINT

COMPANIONS:..

....

INTERESTING SIGHTS

....

....

....

....

....

....

REFLECTIONS FOR JOURNAL

What was the most challenging part of the hike?

How can I better prepare for this next time?

How did I feel physically and mentally during the hike?

Was there anything I wish I had brought or anything that was unnecessary?

Did I set any goals for myself during the hike, and did I achieve them?

Journal / Notes

Snapshot or Trail Doodle

Hiking Log

Hike Details

Day/Date: ....

Location: ....

Trail: ....

Terrain: ....

Start - Latitude: ....

Longitude: ....

Weather

Feel

☐ Warm ....

☐ Cold

☐ Mild ....

Rating: ☆ ☆ ☆ ☆ ☆

Difficulty:

Time - start : .... end : .... expected finish: ....

Duration: .... Distance: ....

Elevation: ....

Route Type: ☐ Circular ☐ Out-and-Back ☐ Point-to-Point

Companions: ....

....

Interesting Sights

....

....

....

....

....

....

Reflections for Journal

What was the most challenging part of the hike?

How can I better prepare for this next time?

How did I feel physically and mentally during the hike?

Was there anything I wish I had brought or anything that was unnecessary?

Did I set any goals for myself during the hike, and did I achieve them?

Journal / Notes

Snapshot or Trail Doodle

Hiking Log

Hike Details

Day/Date:..

Location:..

Trail:..

Terrain:..

Start - Latitude:..

Longitude:..

Weather

Feel

- ☐ Warm ....
- ☐ Cold
- ☐ Mild ....

Rating: ☆ ☆ ☆ ☆ ☆

Difficulty:

Time - start :.................. end :.................. expected finish:................

Duration:.................. **Distance:**..................

Elevation:..

Route Type: ☐ Circular ☐ Out-and-Back ☐ Point-to-Point

Companions:..

....

Interesting Sights

....

....

....

....

....

....

Reflections for Journal

What was the most challenging part of the hike?

How can I better prepare for this next time?

How did I feel physically and mentally during the hike?

Was there anything I wish I had brought or anything that was unnecessary?

Did I set any goals for myself during the hike, and did I achieve them?

Journal / Notes

Snapshot or Trail Doodle

Hiking Log

Hike Details

Day/Date:..

Location:..

Trail:..

Terrain:..

Start - Latitude:..

Longitude:..

Weather

Feel

☐ Warm ....

☐ Cold

☐ Mild ....

Rating: ☆ ☆ ☆ ☆ ☆

Difficulty:

Time - start :.................. end :.................. expected finish:................

Duration:.................. Distance:..................

Elevation:..

Route Type: ☐ Circular ☐ Out-and-Back ☐ Point-to-Point

Companions:..

....

Interesting Sights

....

....

....

....

....

....

Reflections for Journal

What was the most challenging part of the hike?

How can I better prepare for this next time?

How did I feel physically and mentally during the hike?

Was there anything I wish I had brought or anything that was unnecessary?

Did I set any goals for myself during the hike, and did I achieve them?

Journal / Notes

Snapshot or Trail Doodle

Hiking Log

Hike Details

Day/Date: ....

Location: ....

Trail: ....

Terrain: ....

Start - Latitude: ....

Longitude: ....

Weather

Feel

☐ Warm ....

☐ Cold

☐ Mild ....

Rating: ☆ ☆ ☆ ☆ ☆

Difficulty:

Time - start : .... end : .... expected finish: ....

Duration: .... **Distance:** ....

Elevation: ....

Route Type: ☐ Circular ☐ Out-and-Back ☐ Point-to-Point

Companions: ....

....

Interesting Sights

....

....

....

....

....

....

Reflections for Journal

What was the most challenging part of the hike?

How can I better prepare for this next time?

How did I feel physically and mentally during the hike?

Was there anything I wish I had brought or anything that was unnecessary?

Did I set any goals for myself during the hike, and did I achieve them?

Journal / Notes

Snapshot or Trail Doodle

Hiking Log

Hike Details

Day/Date: ....

Location: ....

Trail: ....

Terrain: ....

Start - Latitude: ....

Longitude: ....

Weather

Feel

☐ Warm ....

☐ Cold

☐ Mild ....

Rating: ☆ ☆ ☆ ☆ ☆

Difficulty:

Time - start : .... end : .... expected finish: ....

Duration: .... **Distance:** ....

Elevation: ....

Route Type: ☐ Circular ☐ Out-and-Back ☐ Point-to-Point

Companions: ....

....

Interesting Sights

....

....

....

....

....

....

Reflections for Journal

What was the most challenging part of the hike?

How can I better prepare for this next time?

How did I feel physically and mentally during the hike?

Was there anything I wish I had brought or anything that was unnecessary?

Did I set any goals for myself during the hike, and did I achieve them?

Journal / Notes

Snapshot or Trail Doodle

Hiking Log

Hike Details

Day/Date: ....

Location: ....

Trail: ....

Terrain: ....

Start - Latitude: ....

Longitude: ....

Weather

Feel

- ☐ Warm ....
- ☐ Cold
- ☐ Mild ....

Rating: ☆ ☆ ☆ ☆ ☆

Difficulty:

Time - start : .... end : .... expected finish: ....

Duration: .... **Distance:** ....

Elevation: ....

Route Type: ☐ Circular ☐ Out-and-Back ☐ Point-to-Point

Companions: ....

....

Interesting Sights

....

....

....

....

....

....

Reflections for Journal

What was the most challenging part of the hike?

How can I better prepare for this next time?

How did I feel physically and mentally during the hike?

Was there anything I wish I had brought or anything that was unnecessary?

Did I set any goals for myself during the hike, and did I achieve them?

Journal / Notes

Snapshot or Trail Doodle

Hiking Log

Hike Details

Day/Date: ....

Location: ....

Trail: ....

Terrain: ....

Start - Latitude: ....

Longitude: ....

Weather

Feel

☐ Warm

☐ Cold

☐ Mild

....

....

Rating: ☆ ☆ ☆ ☆ ☆

Difficulty:

Time - start : .... end : .... expected finish: ....

Duration: .... **Distance:** ....

Elevation: ....

Route Type: ☐ Circular ☐ Out-and-Back ☐ Point-to-Point

Companions: ....

....

Interesting Sights

....

....

....

....

....

....

Reflections for Journal

What was the most challenging part of the hike?

How can I better prepare for this next time?

How did I feel physically and mentally during the hike?

Was there anything I wish I had brought or anything that was unnecessary?

Did I set any goals for myself during the hike, and did I achieve them?

Journal / Notes

Snapshot or Trail Doodle

Hiking Log

Hike Details

Day/Date: ....

Location: ....

Trail: ....

Terrain: ....

Start - Latitude: ....

Longitude: ....

Weather

Feel

- ☐ Warm ....
- ☐ Cold
- ☐ Mild ....

Rating: ☆ ☆ ☆ ☆ ☆

Difficulty:

Time - START : .... END : .... EXPECTED FINISH: ....

Duration: .... **Distance:** ....

Elevation: ....

Route Type: ☐ Circular ☐ Out-and-Back ☐ Point-to-Point

Companions: ....

....

Interesting Sights

....

....

....

....

....

....

Reflections for Journal

What was the most challenging part of the hike?

How can I better prepare for this next time?

How did I feel physically and mentally during the hike?

Was there anything I wish I had brought or anything that was unnecessary?

Did I set any goals for myself during the hike, and did I achieve them?

Journal / Notes

Snapshot or Trail Doodle

Hiking Log

Hike Details

Day/Date: ....

Location: ....

Trail: ....

Terrain: ....

Start - Latitude: ....

Longitude: ....

Weather

Feel

- [ ] Warm ....
- [ ] Cold
- [ ] Mild ....

Rating: ☆ ☆ ☆ ☆ ☆

Difficulty:

Time - start : .... end : .... expected finish: ....

Duration: .... **Distance:** ....

Elevation: ....

Route Type: ☐ Circular ☐ Out-and-Back ☐ Point-to-Point

Companions: ....

....

Interesting Sights

....

....

....

....

....

....

Reflections for Journal

What was the most challenging part of the hike?

How can I better prepare for this next time?

How did I feel physically and mentally during the hike?

Was there anything I wish I had brought or anything that was unnecessary?

Did I set any goals for myself during the hike, and did I achieve them?

JOURNAL / NOTES

SNAPSHOT OR TRAIL DOODLE

Hiking Log

Hike Details

Day/Date: ....

Location: ....

Trail: ....

Terrain: ....

Start - Latitude: ....

Longitude: ....

Weather

Feel

☐ Warm

☐ Cold

☐ Mild

....

....

Rating: ☆ ☆ ☆ ☆ ☆

Difficulty:

Time - start : .... end : .... expected finish: ....

Duration: .... **Distance:** ....

Elevation: ....

Route Type: ☐ Circular ☐ Out-and-Back ☐ Point-to-Point

Companions: ....

....

Interesting Sights

....

....

....

....

....

....

Reflections for Journal

What was the most challenging part of the hike?

How can I better prepare for this next time?

How did I feel physically and mentally during the hike?

Was there anything I wish I had brought or anything that was unnecessary?

Did I set any goals for myself during the hike, and did I achieve them?

Journal / Notes

Snapshot or Trail Doodle

Hiking Log

Hike Details

Day/Date: ....

Location: ....

Trail: ....

Terrain: ....

Start - Latitude: ....

Longitude: ....

Weather

Feel

- ☐ Warm ....
- ☐ Cold
- ☐ Mild ....

Rating: ☆ ☆ ☆ ☆ ☆

Difficulty:

Time - START : .... END : .... EXPECTED FINISH: ....

Duration: .... **Distance:** ....

Elevation: ....

Route Type: ☐ Circular ☐ Out-and-Back ☐ Point-to-Point

Companions: ....

....

Interesting Sights

....

....

....

....

....

....

Reflections for Journal

What was the most challenging part of the hike?

How can I better prepare for this next time?

How did I feel physically and mentally during the hike?

Was there anything I wish I had brought or anything that was unnecessary?

Did I set any goals for myself during the hike, and did I achieve them?

Journal / Notes

Snapshot or Trail Doodle

Hiking Log

Hike Details

Day/Date: ....

Location: ....

Trail: ....

Terrain: ....

Start - Latitude: ....

Longitude: ....

Weather

Feel

☐ Warm

☐ Cold

☐ Mild

....

....

Rating: ☆ ☆ ☆ ☆ ☆

Difficulty:

Time - start : .... end : .... expected finish: ....

Duration: .... **Distance:** ....

Elevation: ....

Route Type: ☐ Circular ☐ Out-and-Back ☐ Point-to-Point

Companions: ....

....

Interesting Sights

....

....

....

....

....

....

Reflections for Journal

What was the most challenging part of the hike?

How can I better prepare for this next time?

How did I feel physically and mentally during the hike?

Was there anything I wish I had brought or anything that was unnecessary?

Did I set any goals for myself during the hike, and did I achieve them?

Journal / Notes

Snapshot or Trail Doodle

Hiking Log

Hike Details

Day/Date: ....

Location: ....

Trail: ....

Terrain: ....

Start - Latitude: ....

Longitude: ....

Weather

Feel

☐ Warm ....

☐ Cold

☐ Mild ....

Rating: ☆ ☆ ☆ ☆ ☆

Difficulty:

Time - start : .... end : .... expected finish: ....

Duration: .... **Distance:** ....

Elevation: ....

Route Type: ☐ Circular ☐ Out-and-Back ☐ Point-to-Point

Companions: ....

....

Interesting Sights

....

....

....

....

....

....

Reflections for Journal

What was the most challenging part of the hike?

How can I better prepare for this next time?

How did I feel physically and mentally during the hike?

Was there anything I wish I had brought or anything that was unnecessary?

Did I set any goals for myself during the hike, and did I achieve them?

Journal / Notes

Snapshot or Trail Doodle

Hiking Log

Hike Details

Day/Date: ....

Location: ....

Trail: ....

Terrain: ....

Start - Latitude: ....

Longitude: ....

Weather

Feel

- ☐ Warm ....
- ☐ Cold
- ☐ Mild ....

Rating: ☆ ☆ ☆ ☆ ☆

Difficulty:

Time - start: .... end: .... expected finish: ....

Duration: .... Distance: ....

Elevation: ....

Route Type: ☐ Circular ☐ Out-and-Back ☐ Point-to-Point

Companions: ....

....

Interesting Sights

....

....

....

....

....

....

Reflections for Journal

What was the most challenging part of the hike?

How can I better prepare for this next time?

How did I feel physically and mentally during the hike?

Was there anything I wish I had brought or anything that was unnecessary?

Did I set any goals for myself during the hike, and did I achieve them?

Journal / Notes

Snapshot or Trail Doodle

Progress Update

Go back to the last goal page, reflect on your goals and achievements. How are you progressing? It's helpful to write down the positives and negatives.

Fitness & Endurance

What has helped you get fitter? Can you include these in your routine?

Did you overcome any challenges? What improvements can you make to help realise your goals?

Skills & Knowledge

What new skills have you acquired? How do they help your hiking? How can you improve?

Think about a time when you successfully applied a new skill or knowledge during a hike.

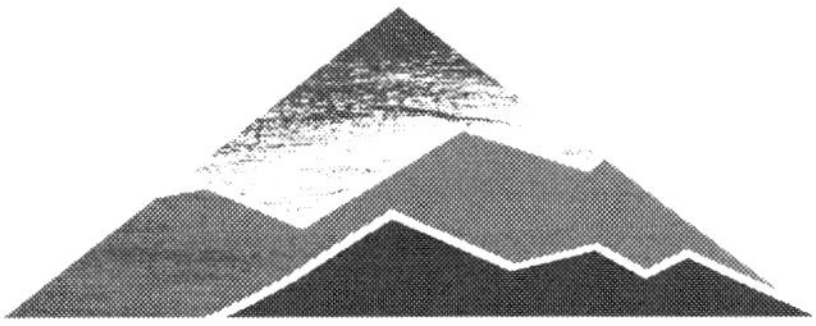

Exploration & Adventure

What new places have you hiked?
What was your most memorable hike?

What challenges or fears have you overcome?
How did you confront them?

Personal Growth & Reflection

Consider hikings' impact on you
What do you notice on hikes more?
What drives you?

What has pushed you out of your comfort zone?
What did you learn about yourself?

HIKING LOG

HIKE DETAILS

DAY/DATE:..

LOCATION:..

TRAIL:..

TERRAIN:..

START - LATITUDE:..

LONGITUDE:..

WEATHER

FEEL

☐ WARM ....

☐ COLD

☐ MILD ....

RATING: ☆ ☆ ☆ ☆ ☆

DIFFICULTY:

TIME - START :.................. END :.................. EXPECTED FINISH:................

DURATION:.................. DISTANCE:..................

ELEVATION:..

ROUTE TYPE: ☐ CIRCULAR ☐ OUT-AND-BACK ☐ POINT-TO-POINT

COMPANIONS:..

....

INTERESTING SIGHTS

....

....

....

....

....

....

REFLECTIONS FOR JOURNAL

What was the most challenging part of the hike?

How can I better prepare for this next time?

How did I feel physically and mentally during the hike?

Was there anything I wish I had brought or anything that was unnecessary?

Did I set any goals for myself during the hike, and did I achieve them?

Journal / Notes

Snapshot or Trail Doodle

Hiking Log

Hike Details

Day/Date: ....

Location: ....

Trail: ....

Terrain: ....

Start - Latitude: ....

Longitude: ....

Weather

Feel

☐ Warm ....

☐ Cold

☐ Mild ....

Rating: ☆ ☆ ☆ ☆ ☆

Difficulty:

Time - start : .... end : .... expected finish: ....

Duration: .... **Distance:** ....

Elevation: ....

Route Type: ☐ Circular ☐ Out-and-Back ☐ Point-to-Point

Companions: ....

....

Interesting Sights

....

....

....

....

....

....

Reflections for Journal

What was the most challenging part of the hike?

How can I better prepare for this next time?

How did I feel physically and mentally during the hike?

Was there anything I wish I had brought or anything that was unnecessary?

Did I set any goals for myself during the hike, and did I achieve them?

Journal / Notes

Snapshot or Trail Doodle

Hiking Log

Hike Details

Day/Date: ....

Location: ....

Trail: ....

Terrain: ....

Start - Latitude: ....

Longitude: ....

Weather

Feel

☐ Warm ....

☐ Cold

☐ Mild ....

Rating: ☆ ☆ ☆ ☆ ☆ **Difficulty:**

Time - start: .... end: .... expected finish: ....

Duration: .... **Distance:** ....

Elevation: ....

Route Type: ☐ Circular ☐ Out-and-Back ☐ Point-to-Point

Companions: ....

....

Interesting Sights

....

....

....

....

....

....

Reflections for Journal

What was the most challenging part of the hike?

How can I better prepare for this next time?

How did I feel physically and mentally during the hike?

Was there anything I wish I had brought or anything that was unnecessary?

Did I set any goals for myself during the hike, and did I achieve them?

Journal / Notes

Snapshot or Trail Doodle

Hiking Log

Hike Details

Day/Date: ....

Location: ....

Trail: ....

Terrain: ....

Start - Latitude: ....

Longitude: ....

Weather

Feel

☐ Warm ....

☐ Cold

☐ Mild ....

Rating: ☆ ☆ ☆ ☆ ☆

Difficulty:

Time - start : .... end : .... expected finish: ....

Duration: .... **Distance:** ....

Elevation: ....

Route Type: ☐ Circular ☐ Out-and-Back ☐ Point-to-Point

Companions: ....

....

Interesting Sights

....

....

....

....

....

....

Reflections for Journal

What was the most challenging part of the hike?

How can I better prepare for this next time?

How did I feel physically and mentally during the hike?

Was there anything I wish I had brought or anything that was unnecessary?

Did I set any goals for myself during the hike, and did I achieve them?

Journal / Notes

Snapshot or Trail Doodle

Hiking Log

Hike Details

Day/Date: ....

Location: ....

Trail: ....

Terrain: ....

Start - Latitude: ....

Longitude: ....

Weather

Feel

☐ Warm

☐ Cold

☐ Mild

....

....

Rating: ☆ ☆ ☆ ☆ ☆

Difficulty:

Time - start : .... end : .... expected finish: ....

Duration: .... **Distance:** ....

Elevation: ....

Route Type: ☐ Circular ☐ Out-and-Back ☐ Point-to-Point

Companions: ....

....

Interesting Sights

....

....

....

....

....

....

Reflections for Journal

What was the most challenging part of the hike?

How can I better prepare for this next time?

How did I feel physically and mentally during the hike?

Was there anything I wish I had brought or anything that was unnecessary?

Did I set any goals for myself during the hike, and did I achieve them?

Journal / Notes

Snapshot or Trail Doodle

Hiking Log

Hike Details

Day/Date: ....

Location: ....

Trail: ....

Terrain: ....

Start - Latitude: ....

Longitude: ....

Weather

Feel

- ☐ Warm ....
- ☐ Cold
- ☐ Mild ....

Rating: ☆ ☆ ☆ ☆ ☆

Difficulty:

Time - start : .... end : .... expected finish: ....

Duration: .... **Distance:** ....

Elevation: ....

Route Type: ☐ Circular ☐ Out-and-Back ☐ Point-to-Point

Companions: ....

....

Interesting Sights

....

....

....

....

....

....

Reflections for Journal

What was the most challenging part of the hike?

How can I better prepare for this next time?

How did I feel physically and mentally during the hike?

Was there anything I wish I had brought or anything that was unnecessary?

Did I set any goals for myself during the hike, and did I achieve them?

Journal / Notes

Snapshot or Trail Doodle

Hiking Log

Hike Details

Day/Date:..

Location:..

Trail:..

Terrain:..

Start - Latitude:..

Longitude:..

Weather

Feel

- [ ] Warm ....
- [ ] Cold
- [ ] Mild ....

Rating: ☆ ☆ ☆ ☆ ☆ **Difficulty:**

Time - START :.................. END :.................... EXPECTED FINISH:................

Duration:.................. **Distance:**..................

Elevation:..

Route Type: ☐ Circular ☐ Out-and-Back ☐ Point-to-Point

Companions:..

....

Interesting Sights

....

....

....

....

....

....

Reflections for Journal

What was the most challenging part of the hike?

How can I better prepare for this next time?

How did I feel physically and mentally during the hike?

Was there anything I wish I had brought or anything that was unnecessary?

Did I set any goals for myself during the hike, and did I achieve them?

Journal / Notes

Snapshot or Trail Doodle

Hiking Log

Hike Details

Day/Date: ....

Location: ....

Trail: ....

Terrain: ....

Start - Latitude: ....

Longitude: ....

Weather

Feel

☐ Warm

☐ Cold ....

☐ Mild ....

Rating: ☆ ☆ ☆ ☆ ☆ **Difficulty:**

Time - START : .... END : .... EXPECTED FINISH: ....

Duration: .... **Distance:** ....

Elevation: ....

Route Type: ☐ Circular ☐ Out-and-Back ☐ Point-to-Point

Companions: ....

....

Interesting Sights

....

....

....

....

....

....

Reflections for Journal

What was the most challenging part of the hike?

How can I better prepare for this next time?

How did I feel physically and mentally during the hike?

Was there anything I wish I had brought or anything that was unnecessary?

Did I set any goals for myself during the hike, and did I achieve them?

Journal / Notes

Snapshot or Trail Doodle

Hiking Log

Hike Details

Day/Date: ....

Location: ....

Trail: ....

Terrain: ....

Start - Latitude: ....

Longitude: ....

Weather

Feel

- [ ] Warm
- [ ] Cold
- [ ] Mild

....

....

Rating: ☆ ☆ ☆ ☆ ☆ **Difficulty:**

Time - start : .... end : .... expected finish: ....

Duration: .... **Distance:** ....

Elevation: ....

Route Type: ☐ Circular ☐ Out-and-Back ☐ Point-to-Point

Companions: ....

....

Interesting Sights

....

....

....

....

....

....

Reflections for Journal

What was the most challenging part of the hike?

How can I better prepare for this next time?

How did I feel physically and mentally during the hike?

Was there anything I wish I had brought or anything that was unnecessary?

Did I set any goals for myself during the hike, and did I achieve them?

Journal / Notes

Snapshot or Trail Doodle

Hiking Log

Hike Details

Day/Date: ....

Location: ....

Trail: ....

Terrain: ....

Start - Latitude: ....

Longitude: ....

Weather

Feel

☐ Warm ....

☐ Cold

☐ Mild ....

Rating: ☆ ☆ ☆ ☆ ☆

Difficulty:

Time - start : .... end : .... expected finish: ....

Duration: .... **Distance:** ....

Elevation: ....

Route Type: ☐ Circular ☐ Out-and-Back ☐ Point-to-Point

Companions: ....

....

Interesting Sights

....

....

....

....

....

....

Reflections for Journal

What was the most challenging part of the hike?

How can I better prepare for this next time?

How did I feel physically and mentally during the hike?

Was there anything I wish I had brought or anything that was unnecessary?

Did I set any goals for myself during the hike, and did I achieve them?

Journal / Notes

Snapshot or Trail Doodle

Hiking Log

Hike Details

Day/Date: ....

Location: ....

Trail: ....

Terrain: ....

Start - Latitude: ....

Longitude: ....

Weather

Feel

☐ Warm ....

☐ Cold

☐ Mild ....

Rating: ☆ ☆ ☆ ☆ ☆

Difficulty:

Time - start : .... end : .... expected finish: ....

Duration: .... **Distance:** ....

Elevation: ....

Route Type: ☐ Circular ☐ Out-and-Back ☐ Point-to-Point

Companions: ....

....

Interesting Sights

....

....

....

....

....

....

Reflections for Journal

What was the most challenging part of the hike?

How can I better prepare for this next time?

How did I feel physically and mentally during the hike?

Was there anything I wish I had brought or anything that was unnecessary?

Did I set any goals for myself during the hike, and did I achieve them?

Journal / Notes

Snapshot or Trail Doodle

Hiking Log

Hike Details

Day/Date: ....

Location: ....

Trail: ....

Terrain: ....

Start - Latitude: ....

Longitude: ....

Weather

Feel

☐ Warm ....

☐ Cold

☐ Mild ....

Rating: ☆ ☆ ☆ ☆ ☆

Difficulty:

Time - start : .... end : .... expected finish: ....

Duration: .... **Distance:** ....

Elevation: ....

Route Type: ☐ Circular ☐ Out-and-Back ☐ Point-to-Point

Companions: ....

....

Interesting Sights

....

....

....

....

....

....

Reflections for Journal

What was the most challenging part of the hike?

How can I better prepare for this next time?

How did I feel physically and mentally during the hike?

Was there anything I wish I had brought or anything that was unnecessary?

Did I set any goals for myself during the hike, and did I achieve them?

Journal / Notes

Snapshot or Trail Doodle

Hiking Log

Hike Details

Day/Date:..

Location:..

Trail:..

Terrain:..

Start - Latitude:..

Longitude:..

Weather

Feel

☐ Warm ....

☐ Cold

☐ Mild ....

Rating: ☆ ☆ ☆ ☆ ☆ **Difficulty:**

Time - start :.................. end :.................. expected finish:................

Duration:.................. **Distance:**..................

Elevation:..

Route Type: ☐ Circular ☐ Out-and-Back ☐ Point-to-Point

Companions:..

....

Interesting Sights

....

....

....

....

....

....

Reflections for Journal

What was the most challenging part of the hike?

How can I better prepare for this next time?

How did I feel physically and mentally during the hike?

Was there anything I wish I had brought or anything that was unnecessary?

Did I set any goals for myself during the hike, and did I achieve them?

Journal / Notes

Snapshot or Trail Doodle

Hiking Log

Hike Details

Day/Date: ....

Location: ....

Trail: ....

Terrain: ....

Start - Latitude: ....

Longitude: ....

Weather

Feel

☐ Warm

☐ Cold

☐ Mild

....

....

Rating: ☆ ☆ ☆ ☆ ☆

Difficulty:

Time - start : .... end : .... expected finish: ....

Duration: .... **Distance:** ....

Elevation: ....

Route Type: ☐ Circular ☐ Out-and-Back ☐ Point-to-Point

Companions: ....

....

Interesting Sights

....

....

....

....

....

....

Reflections for Journal

What was the most challenging part of the hike?

How can I better prepare for this next time?

How did I feel physically and mentally during the hike?

Was there anything I wish I had brought or anything that was unnecessary?

Did I set any goals for myself during the hike, and did I achieve them?

Journal / Notes

Snapshot or Trail Doodle

Hiking Log

Hike Details

Day/Date: ....

Location: ....

Trail: ....

Terrain: ....

Start - Latitude: ....

Longitude: ....

Weather

Feel

☐ Warm ....

☐ Cold

☐ Mild ....

Rating: ☆ ☆ ☆ ☆ ☆

Difficulty:

Time - start : .... end : .... expected finish: ....

Duration: .... **Distance:** ....

Elevation: ....

Route Type: ☐ Circular ☐ Out-and-Back ☐ Point-to-Point

Companions: ....

....

Interesting Sights

....

....

....

....

....

....

Reflections for Journal

What was the most challenging part of the hike?

How can I better prepare for this next time?

How did I feel physically and mentally during the hike?

Was there anything I wish I had brought or anything that was unnecessary?

Did I set any goals for myself during the hike, and did I achieve them?

Journal / Notes

Snapshot or Trail Doodle

Hiking Log

Hike Details

Day/Date: ....

Location: ....

Trail: ....

Terrain: ....

Start - Latitude: ....

Longitude: ....

Weather

Feel

☐ Warm ....

☐ Cold

☐ Mild ....

Rating: ☆ ☆ ☆ ☆ ☆ **Difficulty:**

Time - start : .... end : .... expected finish: ....

Duration: .... **Distance:** ....

Elevation: ....

Route Type: ☐ Circular ☐ Out-and-Back ☐ Point-to-Point

Companions: ....

....

Interesting Sights

....

....

....

....

....

....

Reflections for Journal

What was the most challenging part of the hike?

How can I better prepare for this next time?

How did I feel physically and mentally during the hike?

Was there anything I wish I had brought or anything that was unnecessary?

Did I set any goals for myself during the hike, and did I achieve them?

Journal / Notes

Snapshot or Trail Doodle

HIKING LOG

HIKE DETAILS

DAY/DATE: ....

LOCATION: ....

TRAIL: ....

TERRAIN: ....

START - LATITUDE: ....

LONGITUDE: ....

WEATHER

FEEL

☐ WARM ....

☐ COLD

☐ MILD ....

RATING: ☆ ☆ ☆ ☆ ☆

DIFFICULTY:

TIME - START : .... END : .... EXPECTED FINISH: ....

DURATION: .... **DISTANCE:** ....

ELEVATION: ....

ROUTE TYPE: ☐ CIRCULAR ☐ OUT-AND-BACK ☐ POINT-TO-POINT

COMPANIONS: ....

....

INTERESTING SIGHTS

....

....

....

....

....

....

REFLECTIONS FOR JOURNAL

What was the most challenging part of the hike?

How can I better prepare for this next time?

How did I feel physically and mentally during the hike?

Was there anything I wish I had brought or anything that was unnecessary?

Did I set any goals for myself during the hike, and did I achieve them?

Journal / Notes

Snapshot or Trail Doodle

HIKING LOG

HIKE DETAILS

DAY/DATE:..

LOCATION:..

TRAIL:..

TERRAIN:..

START - LATITUDE:..

LONGITUDE:..

WEATHER

FEEL

- [ ] WARM ....
- [ ] COLD
- [ ] MILD ....

RATING: ☆ ☆ ☆ ☆ ☆

DIFFICULTY:

TIME - START :.................. END :.................. EXPECTED FINISH:................

DURATION:.................. **DISTANCE:**..................

ELEVATION:..

ROUTE TYPE: ☐ CIRCULAR ☐ OUT-AND-BACK ☐ POINT-TO-POINT

COMPANIONS:..

....

INTERESTING SIGHTS

....

....

....

....

....

....

REFLECTIONS FOR JOURNAL

What was the most challenging part of the hike?

How can I better prepare for this next time?

How did I feel physically and mentally during the hike?

Was there anything I wish I had brought or anything that was unnecessary?

Did I set any goals for myself during the hike, and did I achieve them?

Journal / Notes

Snapshot or Trail Doodle

Hiking Log

Hike Details

Day/Date: ....

Location: ....

Trail: ....

Terrain: ....

Start - Latitude: ....

Longitude: ....

Weather

Feel

- [ ] Warm
- [ ] Cold
- [ ] Mild

....

....

Rating: ☆ ☆ ☆ ☆ ☆

Difficulty:

Time - start : .... end : .... expected finish: ....

Duration: .... **Distance:** ....

Elevation: ....

Route Type: [ ] Circular [ ] Out-and-Back [ ] Point-to-Point

Companions: ....

....

Interesting Sights

....

....

....

....

....

....

Reflections for Journal

What was the most challenging part of the hike?

How can I better prepare for this next time?

How did I feel physically and mentally during the hike?

Was there anything I wish I had brought or anything that was unnecessary?

Did I set any goals for myself during the hike, and did I achieve them?

Journal / Notes

Snapshot or Trail Doodle

HIKING LOG

HIKE DETAILS

DAY/DATE:..

LOCATION:..

TRAIL:..

TERRAIN:..

START - LATITUDE:..

LONGITUDE:..

WEATHER

FEEL

- ☐ WARM ....
- ☐ COLD
- ☐ MILD ....

RATING: ☆ ☆ ☆ ☆ ☆

DIFFICULTY:

TIME - START :.................. END :..................... EXPECTED FINISH:...............

DURATION:.................. **DISTANCE:**..................

ELEVATION:...

ROUTE TYPE: ☐ CIRCULAR ☐ OUT-AND-BACK ☐ POINT-TO-POINT

COMPANIONS:..

....

INTERESTING SIGHTS

....

....

....

....

....

....

REFLECTIONS FOR JOURNAL

What was the most challenging part of the hike?

How can I better prepare for this next time?

How did I feel physically and mentally during the hike?

Was there anything I wish I had brought or anything that was unnecessary?

Did I set any goals for myself during the hike, and did I achieve them?

Journal / Notes

Snapshot or Trail Doodle

Progress Update

Go back to the last goal page, reflect on your goals and achievements. How are you progressing? It's helpful to write down the positives and negatives.

Fitness & Endurance

What has helped you get fitter? Can you include these in your routine?

Did you overcome any challenges? What improvements can you make to help realise your goals?

Skills & Knowledge

What new skills have you acquired? How do they help your hiking? How can you improve?

Think about a time when you successfully applied a new skill or knowledge during a hike.

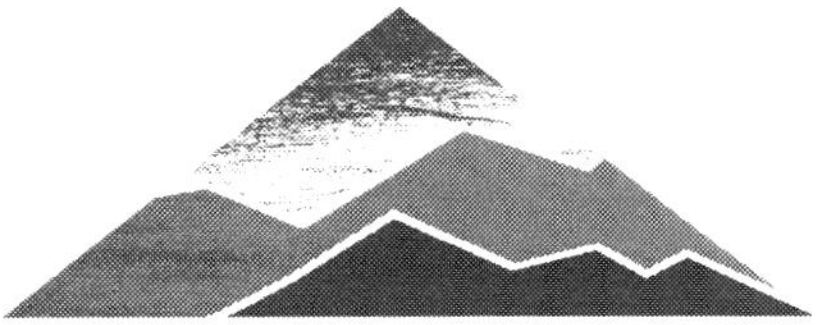

Exploration & Adventure

What new places have you hiked?
What was your most memorable hike?

What challenges or fears have you overcome?
How did you confront them?

Personal Growth & Reflection

Consider hikings' impact on you
What do you notice on hikes more?
What drives you?

What has pushed you out of your comfort zone?
What did you learn about yourself?

Hiking Log

Hike Details

Day/Date: ....

Location: ....

Trail: ....

Terrain: ....

Start - Latitude: ....

Longitude: ....

Weather

Feel

☐ Warm

☐ Cold

☐ Mild

....

....

Rating: ☆ ☆ ☆ ☆ ☆

Difficulty:

Time - start: .... end: .... expected finish: ....

Duration: .... **Distance:** ....

Elevation: ....

Route Type: ☐ Circular ☐ Out-and-Back ☐ Point-to-Point

Companions: ....

....

Interesting Sights

....

....

....

....

....

....

Reflections for Journal

What was the most challenging part of the hike?

How can I better prepare for this next time?

How did I feel physically and mentally during the hike?

Was there anything I wish I had brought or anything that was unnecessary?

Did I set any goals for myself during the hike, and did I achieve them?

Journal / Notes

Snapshot or Trail Doodle

Hiking Log

Hike Details

Day/Date:..

Location:..

Trail:..

Terrain:..

Start - Latitude:..

Longitude:..

Weather

Feel

☐ Warm ....

☐ Cold

☐ Mild ....

Rating: ☆ ☆ ☆ ☆ ☆

Difficulty:

Time - start :.................. end :..................... expected finish:...............

Duration:.................... **Distance:**....................

Elevation:..

Route Type: ☐ Circular ☐ Out-and-Back ☐ Point-to-Point

Companions:..

....

Interesting Sights

....

....

....

....

....

....

Reflections for Journal

What was the most challenging part of the hike?

How can I better prepare for this next time?

How did I feel physically and mentally during the hike?

Was there anything I wish I had brought or anything that was unnecessary?

Did I set any goals for myself during the hike, and did I achieve them?

Journal / Notes

Snapshot or Trail Doodle

Hiking Log

Hike Details

Day/Date: ....

Location: ....

Trail: ....

Terrain: ....

Start - Latitude: ....

Longitude: ....

Weather

Feel

☐ Warm ....

☐ Cold

☐ Mild ....

Rating: ☆ ☆ ☆ ☆ ☆

Difficulty:

Time - start : .... end : .... expected finish: ....

Duration: .... **Distance:** ....

Elevation: ....

Route Type: ☐ Circular ☐ Out-and-Back ☐ Point-to-Point

Companions: ....

....

Interesting Sights

....

....

....

....

....

....

Reflections for Journal

What was the most challenging part of the hike?

How can I better prepare for this next time?

How did I feel physically and mentally during the hike?

Was there anything I wish I had brought or anything that was unnecessary?

Did I set any goals for myself during the hike, and did I achieve them?

Journal / Notes

Snapshot or Trail Doodle

HIKING LOG

HIKE DETAILS

DAY/DATE: ....

LOCATION: ....

TRAIL: ....

TERRAIN: ....

START - LATITUDE: ....

LONGITUDE: ....

WEATHER

FEEL

☐ WARM ....

☐ COLD

☐ MILD ....

RATING: ☆ ☆ ☆ ☆ ☆

DIFFICULTY:

TIME - START : .... END : .... EXPECTED FINISH: ....

DURATION: .... **DISTANCE:** ....

ELEVATION: ....

ROUTE TYPE: ☐ CIRCULAR ☐ OUT-AND-BACK ☐ POINT-TO-POINT

COMPANIONS: ....

....

INTERESTING SIGHTS

....

....

....

....

....

....

REFLECTIONS FOR JOURNAL

What was the most challenging part of the hike?

How can I better prepare for this next time?

How did I feel physically and mentally during the hike?

Was there anything I wish I had brought or anything that was unnecessary?

Did I set any goals for myself during the hike, and did I achieve them?

JOURNAL / NOTES

SNAPSHOT OR TRAIL DOODLE

HIKING LOG

HIKE DETAILS

DAY/DATE: ....

LOCATION: ....

TRAIL: ....

TERRAIN: ....

START - LATITUDE: ....

LONGITUDE: ....

WEATHER

FEEL

☐ WARM ....

☐ COLD

☐ MILD ....

RATING: ☆ ☆ ☆ ☆ ☆

DIFFICULTY:

TIME - START : .... END : .... EXPECTED FINISH: ....

DURATION: .... **DISTANCE:** ....

ELEVATION: ....

ROUTE TYPE: ☐ CIRCULAR ☐ OUT-AND-BACK ☐ POINT-TO-POINT

COMPANIONS: ....

....

INTERESTING SIGHTS

....

....

....

....

....

....

REFLECTIONS FOR JOURNAL

What was the most challenging part of the hike?

How can I better prepare for this next time?

How did I feel physically and mentally during the hike?

Was there anything I wish I had brought or anything that was unnecessary?

Did I set any goals for myself during the hike, and did I achieve them?

Journal / Notes

Snapshot or Trail Doodle

Hiking Log

Hike Details

Day/Date: ....

Location: ....

Trail: ....

Terrain: ....

Start - Latitude: ....

Longitude: ....

Weather

Feel

- [ ] Warm ....
- [ ] Cold
- [ ] Mild ....

Rating: ☆ ☆ ☆ ☆ ☆

Difficulty:

Time - START : .... END : .... EXPECTED FINISH: ....

Duration: .... **Distance:** ....

Elevation: ....

Route Type: ☐ Circular ☐ Out-and-Back ☐ Point-to-Point

Companions: ....

....

Interesting Sights

....

....

....

....

....

....

Reflections for Journal

What was the most challenging part of the hike?

How can I better prepare for this next time?

How did I feel physically and mentally during the hike?

Was there anything I wish I had brought or anything that was unnecessary?

Did I set any goals for myself during the hike, and did I achieve them?

Journal / Notes

Snapshot or Trail Doodle

Hiking Log

Hike Details

Day/Date: ....

Location: ....

Trail: ....

Terrain: ....

Start - Latitude: ....

Longitude: ....

Weather

Feel

☐ Warm ....

☐ Cold

☐ Mild ....

Rating: ☆ ☆ ☆ ☆ ☆ **Difficulty:**

Time - START : .... END : .... EXPECTED FINISH: ....

Duration: .... **Distance:** ....

Elevation: ....

Route Type: ☐ Circular ☐ Out-and-Back ☐ Point-to-Point

Companions: ....

....

Interesting Sights

....

....

....

....

....

....

Reflections for Journal

What was the most challenging part of the hike?

How can I better prepare for this next time?

How did I feel physically and mentally during the hike?

Was there anything I wish I had brought or anything that was unnecessary?

Did I set any goals for myself during the hike, and did I achieve them?

Journal / Notes

Snapshot or Trail Doodle

Trail Recommendations

Record new paths and share your favorites

TRAIL NAME	LOCATION	NOTES

Trail Name	Location	Notes

PURSUIT JOURNALS

Printed in Great Britain
by Amazon

f05aabc4-3110-457a-9df8-60b35b063d64R01